GIFT

100 readings
in celebration of
birth and parenthood

compiled by
Robert Atwell

CANTERBURY
PRESS
Norwich

© in this compilation Robert Atwell 2005

First published in 2005 by the Canterbury Press Norwich
(a publishing imprint of Hymns Ancient & Modern Limited,
a registered charity)
9–17 St Albans Place, London N1 0NX

www.scm-canterburypress.co.uk

British Library Cataloguing in Publication data

A catalogue record for this book is available
from the British Library

ISBN 1-85311-640-8

Typeset by Regent Typesetting, London
Printed and bound by
Creative Print and Design

Contents

Introduction

The birth of a child is one of the most wonderful moments in life. First the conception, then the development of the foetus in the womb, and finally the birth itself in all its painful messy glory: the entire process is truly miraculous. I never cease to be moved by the sight of a baby's hands, and particularly its fingernails. They are so tiny, and yet so exquisitely shaped, so perfect. For me they encapsulate the miracle not simply of birth, but of life itself.

In my experience a birth brings out the best in people, and can even cause a second miracle to happen, but this time in the lives of those who gather to share in it. As people give thanks for the safe delivery of the child and recovery of its mother, for the gift of new life, their hearts grow bigger. They find themselves smiling on the world. Even the cynical and hard-hearted find it difficult not to be moved by the sight of a newborn baby. Thanksgiving makes us bigger and better people.

Birth is a vulnerable, precarious business, in spite of modern medicine and good pre- and post-natal care. There is relief as well as joy when a baby emerges from the womb. And as we all know, although the birth of a child is momentous, it is only the first event in what will evolve into the long saga of parenting. And parenting is neither easy nor necessarily all wonderful. In the years that lie ahead there will be joys to be shared, birthdays and milestones to be celebrated, but there will also be difficulties and problems to be overcome. All parenting includes a good deal of both heartache and headache as babies become toddlers, toddlers grow into children, and children turn into stroppy teenagers. Finally, as teenagers become young adults, parenting requires a letting-go as profound as when the umbilical cord was severed at birth. In the words of C. Day Lewis, 'selfhood begins with a walking away, and love is proved in the letting go'. Occasionally, parenting also includes the sadness of a child becoming sick or even terminally ill. The death of a child is a trauma that few families ever completely recover from. Mercifully, it is something that rarely happens (at least in the West), but the fear of it haunts every parent and grandparent.

The gift of a child is cause for celebration in every culture and in every age. The naming of a child, a christening, the recovery of the mother after childbirth and her return home, are all important occasions in the life of a family, and over the ages have been marked by various rites and ceremonies. They are moments and events which have also generated all sorts of poems, songs and reflections. Those assembled here are just the tip of an iceberg. As a selection of readings they move from conception, through birth and baptism to childhood. They can be used as a resource for readings at a naming ceremony or baptism, or just to curl up with in an armchair and browse in an odd quiet moment. Taken individually or collectively, they remind us how precious the gift of life is, and how we do well not to squander it.

Robert Atwell

Bringing to birth

Lovesong
to an unborn child

The water is wide and smooth in Galway Bay,
    bright, as if mirrored more than sky.
I want to be close to you. I want so much to know

your secret beauty, darling of my heart.
Whom shall I tell who knows what you are like
if not this sea, and clouds, ephemeral?

And changing as your forms and these grey shrimp,
almost invisible in the puckered pools,
as small as you are early in your day.

I am involved in correspondences
to know you. I can see this face,
his gold-ringed eyes, his wet and glistening skin

and this my own, remelted in the real.
I drift in the water, as do you.
Soon, you will reach out, my love, to touch me.

The wavelets lap and chill. He wades to meet me,
smiles, glides away. I sense partings
more terrible than this, returning

once or twice a year, photographs.
Is it better then to tell only
clouds, shrimp and passing waves who know

how to keep secrets; none so deep as love
unspoken, unrevealed? I do not know
if I sink or swim. O Waly, Waly.

Anne Richards

[3]

Lord, you have searched me out and known me

Lord, you have created my inmost being,
knitting me together in my mother's womb.
I will thank you, O God, for I am wonderfully made.
Your deeds are wonderful and your works marvellous.

You watched every bone taking shape,
forming in the hidden depths.
You saw my limbs growing
and shaped my body according to your design.

How deep are your thoughts to me, O God!
How vast is their sum!
Were I to try and count them,
they would be more than the grains of sand upon the
seashore.

Search me out, O God, and know my heart;
test me and examine my thoughts.
Look and see if there is any wickedness in me,
and lead me in the way that is everlasting.

Psalm 139, the Bible

My heart leaps up when I behold

My heart leaps up when I behold
    A rainbow in the sky:
So it was when my life began;
So it is now I am a man;
So be it when I shall grow old,
    Or let me die!
The Child is father of the Man;
And I could wish my days to be
Bound each to each by natural piety.

William Wordsworth (1770–1850)

The year's at the spring

The year's at the spring,
    And day's at the morn;
Morning's at seven;
The hill-side's dew-pearled;
The lark's on the wing;
The snail's on the thorn:
God's in his heaven –
All's right with the world!

Robert Browning (1812–89), *Pippa Passes*

Spring

Nothing is so beautiful as spring –
  When weeds, in wheels, shoot long and
  lovely and lush;
  Thrush's eggs look little low heavens, and
  thrush
Through the echoing timber does so rinse and wring
The ear, it strikes like lightnings to hear him sing;
  The glassy peartree leaves and blooms, they
  brush
  The descending blue; that blue is all in a rush
With richness; the racing lambs too have fair their fling.

What is all this juice and all this joy?
  A strain of the earth's sweet being in the
  beginning
In Eden garden. – Have, get, before it cloy,
  Before it cloud, Christ, lord, and sour with
  sinning,
Innocent mind and Mayday in girl and boy,
  Most, O maid's child, thy choice and worthy
  the winning.

Gerard Manley Hopkins (1844–89)

Pied beauty

Glory be to God for dappled things –
　　For skies of couple-colour as a brinded cow;
　　　　For rose-moles all in stipple upon trout
　　　　that swim;
Fresh-firecoal chestnut-falls; finches' wings;
　　Landscape plotted and pieced – fold, fallow, and
　　plough;
　　　　And áll trádes, their gear and tackle and
　　　　trim.

All things counter, original, spare, strange;
　　Whatever is fickle, freckled (who knows how?)
　　　　With swift, slow; sweet, sour; adazzle, dim;
He fathers-forth whose beauty is past change:
　　　　　　　　　　　　　　　　Praise him

Gerard Manley Hopkins (1844–89)

Every conception is immaculate

It has always seemed to me that every conception is immaculate and that this dogma concerning the Mother of God expresses the idea of all motherhood. At the moment of childbirth, every woman has the same aura of isolation, as though she were abandoned, alone. At this vital moment the man's part is as irrelevant as if he had never had anything to do with it, as though the whole thing was gratuitous.

It is the woman, by herself, who brings forth her progeny, and carries it upstairs, to some top story of life, a quiet, safe place for a cradle. Alone, in silence and humility, she feels and rears the child.

The Mother of God is asked to 'pray zealously to her Son and her God' and the words of the psalm are put into her mouth: 'My soul doth magnify the Lord and my spirit hath rejoiced in God my Saviour. For he hath regarded the low estate of his handmaiden: for behold, from henceforth all generations shall call me blessed.' It is because of her child that she says this. He will magnify her ('for he that is mighty hath done to me great things'). He is her glory.

Any woman could say it. For every one of them, God is in her child. Mothers of great men must have this feeling particularly, but then, at the beginning, all women are mothers of great men – it isn't their fault if life disappoints them later.

Boris Pasternak (1890–1960), *Dr Zhivago*

Before the birth of one of her children

All things within this fading world hath end,
  Adversity doth still our joys attend;
No ties so strong, no friends so dear and sweet,
But with death's parting blow is sure to meet.
The sentence past is most irrevocable,
A common thing, yet oh inevitable.
How soon, my dear, death may my steps attend,
How soon't may be thy lot to lose thy friend,
We are both ignorant, yet love bids me
These farewell lines to recommend to thee,
That when that knot's untied that made us one,
I may seem thine, who in effect am none.
And if I see not half my days that's due,
What nature would, God grant to yours and you;
The many faults that well you know I have
Let be interr'd in my oblivious grave;
If any worth or virtue were in me,
Let that live freshly in thy memory
And when thou feel'st no grief, as I no harms,
Yet love thy dead, who long lay in thine arms.
And when thy loss shall be repaid with gains
Look to my little babes, my dear remains.
And if thou love thyself, or loved'st me,
These o protect from step dames injury.
And if chance to thine eyes shall bring this verse,
With some sad sighs honour my absent hearse;
And kiss this paper for thy loves dear sake,
Who with salt tears this last farewell did take.

Anne Bradstreet (1612–72)

Childbirth

Come to my aid
    Sweet Mary and Bride,
As Anna bore Mary,
As Eile bore John the Baptist,
As Mary bore Christ,
And perfect he was
From quickening to birth.
Help me bear this child,
Help me bring it to life,
Great is my travail,
Help me, O Bride.

Carmina Gadelica

This poem from the Isles of the Hebrides, off the west coast of Scotland, would have been chanted by a woman in labour. 'Anna' is St Anne, mother of the Blessed Virgin Mary; 'Eile' is St Elizabeth, the mother of John the Baptist; and 'Bride' is St Brigid. Bride was widely honoured in the Celtic Church, and among other things was the patron saint of 'Aid-women' because of her reputed skill in midwifery.

An ancient aid-woman's prayer

Behold, O Mother Mary,
  This woman near to death,
And Jesus, Son of Mary,
Have mercy on her now:
Give her rest from labour
And bring the child to life.

Dear Christ, look upon her,
Deliver her from death,
You alone possess the power,
You only are the King of health:
Let the little vine-shoot rest
And give its mother peace.

Carmina Gadelica

This prayer from the Isles would have been sung by the aid-woman (midwife) helping a woman in labour.

Where did you come from, baby dear?

Where did you come from, baby dear?
    Out of the everywhere into here.

Where did you get your eyes so blue?
Out of the sky as I came through.

What makes the light in them sparkle and spin?
Some of the starry spikes left in.

Where did you get that little tear?
I found it waiting when I got here.

What makes your forehead so smooth and high?
A soft hand stroked it as I went by.

What makes your cheek like a warm white rose?
I saw something better than anyone knows.

Whence that three-cornered smile of bliss?
Three angels gave me at once a kiss.

Where did you get this pearly ear?
God spoke, and it came out to hear.

Where did you get those arms and hands?
Love made itself into hooks and bands.

Feet, whence did you come, you darling things?
From the same box as the cherubs' wings.

How did they all just come to be you?
God thought about me, and so I grew.

But how did you come to us, you dear?
God thought about you, and so I am here.

George MacDonald (1824–1905)

Birth

Infant sorrow

My mother groaned! My father wept.
    Into the dangerous world I leapt:
Helpless, naked, piping loud;
Like a friend hid in a cloud.

Struggling in my father's hands:
Striving against my swaddling bands:
Bound and weary I thought best
To sulk upon my mother's breast.

William Blake (1757–1827)

Love me

Love me, I love you,
    Love me, my baby;
Sing it high, sing it low,
    Sing it as may be.

Mother's arms under you,
    Her eyes above you
Sing it high, sing it low,
    Love me, I love you.

Christina Rossetti (1830–94)

The precariousness of birth
Monday 9th October 1775

My wife, having been seized with her pains in the night, I got up about three o'clock, and between four and five Dr Young came. He and I sat upstairs mostly till between three and four in the afternoon, when, after we had dined, her labour became violent. I was full of expectation, and meditated curiously on the thought that it was already certain of what sex the child was, but that I could not have the least guess on which side the probability was.

I did not feel so much anxiety about my wife now as on former occasions, being better used to an in-lying. Yet the danger was as great now as ever. I was easier from the same deception which affects a soldier who has escaped several battles. She was very ill. Between seven and eight I went into the room. She was just delivered. I heard her say, 'God be thanked for whatever he sends.' I supposed then the child was a daughter. But she herself had not then seen it. Miss Preston said, 'Is it a daughter?' 'No,' said Mrs Forrest, the nurse-keeper, 'it's a son.' When I had seen the little man I said that I should now be so anxious that probably I should never again have an easy hour!

That night I wrote several letters to announce my son's birth, and I indulged some imaginations that he might perhaps be a great man.

James Boswell (1740–95), from his *Diary*

New arrival

You, who were twice blessed,
    meet a sun which might
never have shone, flowers
that might not have looked at you;
and we see a bud which might
never have been unfurled.

How can we offer thanks
for you who were handed back tenderly;
thanks for this loaning –
the borrowing to love?

Only by hours and the years
not taken for granted,
and by a remembrance
of what might never have been.

Cecily Taylor

The angel that presided o'er my birth

The Angel that presided o'er my birth
    Said, 'Little creature, form'd of joy and mirth,
Go love without the help of any thing on earth.'

William Blake (1757–1827)

The birthnight
to his daughter, Florence

Dearest, it was a night
    That in its darkness rocked Orion's stars;
A sighing wind ran faintly white
Along the willows, and the cedar boughs
Laid their wide hands in stealthy peace across
The starry silence of their antique moss:
No sound save rushing air
Cold, yet all sweet with Spring,
And in thy mother's arms, crouched weeping there,
    Thou, lovely thing.

Walter de la Mare (1873–1956)

Ode

Our birth is but a sleep and a forgetting:
    The Soul that rises with us, our life's Star,
Hath had elsewhere its setting,
    And cometh from afar:
    Not in entire forgetfulness,
    And not in utter nakedness,
But trailing clouds of glory do we come
From God, who is our home:
Heaven lies about us in our infancy!
Shades of the prison-house begin to close
Upon the growing Boy

But he beholds the light, and whence it flows,
He sees it in his joy;
The Youth, who daily farther from the east
Must travel, still is Nature's Priest,
And by the vision splendid
Is on his way attended;
At length the Man perceives it die away,
And fade into the light of common day.

William Wordsworth (1770–1850),
Ode: Intimations of Immortality

The birthing

B ut she had seen the cattle drop their young,
their matted hairy flanks soaked with sweat
bony legs shaking. Their milky eyes sought hers,
a swirl of colour, of dumb question. Into the dung
and the saw of heavy breaths, blind and wet,
the calves somersaulted, head over heels,
skinny arms and legs crumpled together.
They lay against the cows' warm, trembling sides.
What had that ferment to do with her,
so secret, so alone, a separate creature?
Her small belly fattened, the breasts he had taught
    her were beautiful
swelled like melons, the nipples darkened. A
    turmoil
churned inside her, sharp and hard, a sack
of quarrelling pullets, something all bone and beak.

Something of her, but alien. The first pain
rippled across her like a caress, so fleetingly
it fell. From her ankles a blush rose and branched
to all parts of her body. She panted, splashing
cold water onto her face from a stream. Crouched
in the shade of a bush she felt the waves begin.
She breathed with them. Once, under her feet,
the earth had billowed that way, rumbled, shifted,
then rent, dislodging the trees. Her nails bit the
    cheeks
of her palms. What was this uprooting, this quake?
Her limbs flew from her centre, suddenly struck
in a black cataclysm, a flick that cleft
her two parts. She fell, fell into the wound.
It was this she had waited for, His transfixing
    hand!

Beth Bentley

Dear child whom I begot

Dear child whom I begot,
    Forgive if my page
Hymns not your helpless age,
For you are mine, and not:
Mine as sower and sown,
But in yourself your own.

J. V. Cunningham (1911–85)

The miracle of birth

Human beings, preoccupied with our own petty agendas, have lost the capacity to contemplate the works of God by which we should daily render praise to God as Creator. This is why God has, as it were, reserved to himself certain extraordinary and unexpected actions, which we term miracles, in order that by such marvels he might startle people out of their lethargy into worship.

In the Gospel we learn that a dead man called Lazarus rose again, and people marvelled. What amazes me is that numerous babies are born every day, and no one marvels. If only we would reflect upon life more carefully, we would come to see that it is a greater miracle for a child to be given existence who before did not exist, than for a man to come back to life who already existed. People hold cheap what they see every day of their lives, but suddenly, confronted by extraordinary events, they are dumbfounded, though these events are truly no more wonderful than the others.

St Augustine (354–430),
from a commentary on St John's Gospel

Birth

I didn't ask
to be born.
I wasn't even
there to ask.
When you are born
you can ask for
anything.
Almost anything.
You cannot ask
to be unborn.
If you do
there is very little
that can be done.
I didn't ask
to be born.
I was under age
at the time.
My parents had
to decide
on my behalf.
I'm glad that
I was born.
You have to be born
to be glad.

Anonymous

The birth of the Christ-child

God of the moon, God of the sun,
God of the world, God of the stars,
God of the waters, the land, the skies,
Who sent us the King of promise.

Mary knelt to do your will,
Her child was born, the King of Life,
Darkness and tears were left behind,
And the bright star rose to guide us.

It shone on the land, it shone on the sea,
On storm and calm at the water's edge,
Grief was no more, and joy prevailed,
And the world was filled with music.

Carmina Gadelica

Thanksgiving of women after childbirth

Almighty God, we give thee humble thanks for that
thou hast vouchsafed to deliver this woman thy
servant from the great pain and peril of childbirth.
Grant, we beseech thee, most merciful Father, that she,
through thy help, may both faithfully live and walk
according to thy will in this life present; and also may be
partaker of everlasting glory in the life to come; through
Jesus Christ our Lord.

The Churching of Women, from *Book of Common Prayer*,
1662

[23]

Birth of a child

The birth began with a silent splash,
my womb weeping.
The crown of the baby's head
opened my body
like a camera lens
photographing the end of our union.
A doctor's hands
as large as the child's torso
freed the right shoulder,
then the left,
allowing the wet, slippery little boy
to burst forth.
He was laid like a gift on my breast.
Our hearts' duet continued.
My heart would not stop
pumping our blood
through the thick blue braid of veins,
my pulse pounding like a fist
to protest the sterile scissors
cutting our connection.

Shelly Wagner

Surprised by love

The midwife asked me if I would like to see the child. 'Please,' I said gratefully, and she went away and came back with my daughter wrapped up in a small grey bloodstained blanket, and with a ticket saying 'Stacey' round her ankle. She put her in my arms and I sat there looking at her, and her great wide blue eyes looked at me with seeming recognition, and what I felt it is pointless to try to describe. Love, I suppose one might call it, and the first of my life.

I had expected so little, really. I never expect much. I had been told of the ugliness of newborn children, of their red and wrinkled faces, their waxy covering, their emaciated limbs, their hairy cheeks, their piercing cries. All I can say is that mine was beautiful and in my defence I must add that others said she was beautiful too. She was not red nor even wrinkled, but palely soft, each feature delicately posed in its right place, and she was not bald but adorned with a thick, startling crop of black hair. One of the nurses fetched a brush and flattened it down and it covered her forehead, lying in a dense fringe that reached to her eyes. And her eyes, that seemed to see me and that looked into mine with deep gravity and charm, were a profound blue, the whites white with the gleam of alarming health.

Margaret Drabble (1939–), *The Millstone*

Children of the Spirit

Nicodemus asked Jesus, 'How can anyone be born again after having grown old? Can one enter a second time into a mother's womb and be born?' Jesus said to him, 'Very truly, I tell you, no one can enter the kingdom of God without being born of water and Spirit. What is born of the flesh is flesh, and what is born of the Spirit is spirit. Do not be astonished that I said to you, 'You must be born from above. The wind blows where it chooses, and you hear the sound of it, but you do not know where it comes from or where it goes. So it is with everyone who is born of the Spirit.'

St John's Gospel 3.2–8, the Bible

Babies

More babies

'Nothing grows in our garden, only washing. And babies. And where's their fathers live, my love? Over the hills and far away. You're looking up at me now. I know what you're thinking, you poor little milky creature. You're thinking, you're no better than you should be, Polly, and that's good enough for me. Oh, isn't life a terrible thing, thank God?'

Dylan Thomas (1914–53), *Under Milk Wood*

A baby's hands

A baby's hands, like rosebuds furled
　Whence yet no leaf expands,
Open if you touch, though close upcurled,
A baby's hands.

Then, fast as warriors grip their brands
When battle's bolt is hurled,
They close, clenched hard like tightening bands.

No rosebuds yet by dawn impearled
Match, even in loveliest lands,
The sweetest flowers in all the world –
A baby's hands.

Algernon Charles Swinburne (1837–1909)

To Miss Charlotte Pulteney
in her mother's arms

Timely blossom, infant fair,
        Fondling of a happy pair,
Every morn and every night,
Their solicitous delight,
Sleeping, waking, still at ease,
Pleasing, without skill to please,
Little gossip, blithe and hale,
Tattling many a broken tale,
Singing many a tuneless song,
Lavish of a heedless tongue,
Simple maiden, void of art,
Babbling out the very heart,
Yet abandoned to thy will,
Yet imagining no ill,
Yet too innocent to blush,
Like the linlet in the bush,
To the mother-linnet's note
Moduling her slender throat,
Chirping forth thy petty joys,
Wanton in the change of toys,
Like the linnet green in May,
Flitting to each bloomy spray,
Wearied then, glad to rest,
Like the linlet in the nest.
This thy present happy lot,
This, in time, will be forgot:
Other pleasures, other cares,

Ever-busy time prepares;
And thou shalt in thy daughter see
This picture, once, resembled thee.

Ambrose Philips (1674–1749)

To an infant daughter

Sweet gem of infant fairy-flowers!
    Thy smiles on life's unclosing hours,
Like sunbeams lost in summer showers.
        They wake my fears;
When reason knows its sweets and sours,
        They'll change to tears.

God help thee, little senseless thing!
Thou, daisy-like of early spring
Of ambush'd winter's hornet sting
        Hast yet to tell;
Thou know'st not what tomorrows bring
        I wish thee well.

But thou art come, and soon or late
'Tis thine to meet the frowns of fate,
The harpy grin of envy's hate,
        And mermaid-smiles
Of worldly folly's luring bait,
        That youth beguiles.

And much I wish, whate'er may be
The lot, my child, that falls to thee,
Nature may never let thee see
    Her glass betimes
But keep thee from my failings free –
    Nor itch at rhymes.

Lord help thee in thy coming years
If thy mad father's picture 'pears
Predominant! – his feeling fears
    And jingling starts;
I'd freely now gi' vent to tears
    To ease my heart.

May thou, unknown to rhyming bother,
Be ignorant as is thy mother,
And in thy manners such another,
    Save sin's nigh quest;
And then with 'scaping this and t'other
    Thou mayst be blest.

Lord knows my heart, it loves thee much:
And may my feelings, aches, and such,
The pains I meet in folly's clutch
    Be never thine:
Child, it's a tender string to touch,
    That sounds 'Thou'rt mine'.

John Clare (1793–1864)

Infant joy

'I have no name:
    I am but two days old.'
What shall I call thee?
'I happy am,
Joy is my name.'
Sweet joy befall thee!

Pretty joy!
Sweet joy but two days old,
Sweet joy I call thee:
Thou dost smile,
I sing the while,
Sweet joy befall thee!

William Blake (1757–1827), *Songs of Innocence*

I know a baby

I know a baby, such a baby –
    Round blue eyes and cheeks of pink,
Such an elbow furrowed with dimples,
Such a wrist where creases sink.

'Cuddle and love me, cuddle and love me,'
Crows the mouth of coral pink:
Oh the bald head, and oh the sweet lips,
And oh the sleepy eyes that wink!

Christina Rossetti (1830–94)

Gentle whisper, hardly crying

Gentle whisper, hardly crying,
  downy hair and tiny nose,
hold her, sense *her* peaceful movement,
cuddled in *her* baby clothes.

N we love you, darling,
consummation of our dreams.
Ended, weeks of hopeful waiting,
love cascades, and comfort streams.

Praise to God! We offer glory
for the baby that we bring;
born within our family's story,
joy will fill the song we sing.

Birth of hope, our jubilation,
child of all our dreams and plans;
here we hold love's expectation,
priceless treasure in our hands.

May we love *her*, and through loving
bond together, grow and learn;
then through mutual understanding
share this joy we could not earn.

Andrew Pratt

To Ianthe

I love thee, Baby! For thine own sweet sake;
    Those azure eyes, that faintly dimpled cheek.
    Thy tender frame, so eloquently weak,
    Love in the sternest heart of hate might wake;
But more when o'er thy fitful slumber bending
    Thy mother folds thee to her wakeful heart,
    Whilst love and pity, in her glances bending,
    All that thy passive eyes can feel impart:
More, when some feeble lineaments of her,
    Who bore thy weight beneath her spotless
    bosom,
    As with deep love I read thy face, recur! –
More dear thou, O fair and fragile blossom;
    Dearest when most thy tender traits express
    The image of thy mother's loveliness.

Percy Bysshe Shelley (1792–1822)

Frost at midnight

Dear Babe, that sleepest cradled by my side,
    Whose gentle breathings, heard in this deep
    calm,
Fill up the interspersèd vacancies
And momentary pauses of the thought!
My babe so beautiful! It thrills my heart
With tender gladness, thus to look at thee,
And think that thou shalt learn far other lore,

And in far other scenes! for I was reared
In the great city, pent 'mid cloisters dim,
And saw nought lovely but the sky and stars.
But *thou*, my babe! shalt wander like a breeze
By lakes and sandy shores, beneath the crags
Of ancient mountain, and beneath the clouds,
Which image in their bulk both lakes and shores
And mountain crags: so shalt thou see and hear
The lovely shapes and sounds intelligible
Of that eternal language, which thy God
Utters, who from eternity doth teach
Himself in all, and all things in himself.
Great universal Teacher! he shall mould
Thy spirit, and by giving make it ask.
Therefore all seasons shall be sweet to thee,
Whether the summer clothe the general earth
With greenness, or the redbreast sit and sing
Betwixt the tufts of snow on the bare branch
Of mossy apple tree, while the nigh thatch
Smokes in the sun-thaw; whether the eave-drops fall
Heard only in the trances of the blast,
Or if the secret ministry of frost
Shall hang them up in silent icicles,
Quietly shining to the quiet Moon.

Samuel Taylor Coleridge (1772–1834)

A cradle song

Sweet dreams, form a shade
O'er my lovely infant's head;
Sweet dreams of pleasant streams
By happy, silent, moony beams.

Sweet sleep, with soft down
Weave thy brows an infant crown.
Sweet sleep, Angel mild,
Hover o'er my happy child.

Sweet smiles, in the night
Hover over my delight;
Sweet smiles, Mother's smiles,
All the livelong night beguiles.

Sweet moans, dovelike sighs,
Chase not slumber from thy eyes.
Sweet moans, sweeter smiles,
All the dovelike moans beguiles.

Sleep, sleep, happy child,
All creation slept and smil'd;
Sleep, sleep, happy sleep,
While o'er thee thy mother weep.

Sweet babe, in thy face
Holy image I can trace.
Sweet babe, once like thee,
Thy maker lay and wept for me,

Wept for me, for thee, for all,
When he was an infant small.
Thou his image ever see,
Heavenly face that smiles on thee,

Smiles on thee, on me, on all;
Who became an infant small.
Infant smiles are his own smiles;
Heaven and earth to peace beguiles.

William Blake (1757–1827), *Songs of Innocence*

Lord, I have calmed and stilled my soul

L ord, my heart is not proud;
holding my head too high.

I do not busy myself in great matters,
or in things that are beyond me.

Instead I have calmed and stilled my soul,
like a weaned child on its mother's breast;
so is my whole being at rest.

O Israel, trust in the Lord,
from this time forth and for evermore.

Psalm 131, the Bible

A father's lullaby

'Lullaby, oh, lullaby!'
Thus I heard a father cry,
'Lullaby, oh, lullaby!
That brat will never shut an eye;
Hither come, some power divine!
Close his lids or open mine!'

'Lullaby, oh, lullaby!'
What the devil makes him cry?
'Lullaby, oh, lullaby!'
Still he stares – I wonder why?
Why are not the sons of earth
Blind, like puppies, from the birth?

'Lullaby, oh, lullaby!'
Thus I heard the father cry;
'Lullaby, oh, lullaby!
Mary, you must come and try! –
Hush, oh, hush, for mercy's sake –
The more I sing, the more you wake!'

'Lullaby, oh, lullaby!
Two such nights, and I shall die!
Lullaby, oh, lullaby!
He'll be bruised, and so shall I –
How can I from bedposts keep,
When I'm walking in my sleep?'

Thomas Hood (1799–1845)

Letter to Daniel

written by Fergal Keane to his young son,
February 1996

My dear son,

It is six o'clock in the morning on the island of Hong Kong. You are asleep cradled in my left arm and I am learning the art of one-handed typing. Your mother, more tired yet more happy than I've ever known her, is sound asleep in the room next door and there is soft quiet in our apartment.

Since you've arrived, days have melted into night and back again and we are learning a new grammar, a long sentence whose punctuation marks are feeding and winding and nappy changing and these occasional moments of quiet.

When you're older we'll tell you that you were born in Britain's last Asian colony in the lunar year of the pig and that when we brought you home, the staff of our apartment block gathered to wish you well. 'It's a boy, so lucky, so lucky. We Chinese love boys,' they told us. One man said you were the first baby to be born in the block in the year of the pig. This, he told us, was good *Feng Shui*, in other words a positive sign for the building and everyone who lived there.

Naturally your mother and I were only too happy to believe that. We had wanted you and waited for you, imagined you and dreamed about you and now that you are here no dream can do justice to you.

Your coming has turned me upside down and inside

out. So much that seemed essential to me has, in the past few days, taken on a different colour. Like many foreign correspondents I know, I have lived a life that, on occasion, has veered close to the edge: war zones, natural disasters, darkness in all its shapes and forms.

In a world of insecurity and ambition and ego, it's easy to be drawn in, to take chances with our lives, to believe that what we do and what people say about us is reason enough to gamble with death. Now, looking at your sleeping face, inches away from me, listening to your occasional sigh and gurgle, I wonder how I could have ever thought glory and prizes and praise were sweeter than life.

Fergal Keane (1961–)

Letter to Meg
written by Sir Thomas More from the Tower of London to his daughter in 1535

Although, Margaret, I know well that my wickedness has been such that I know myself well worthy that God should let me slip, yet can I not but trust in his merciful goodness that as his grace has strengthened me hitherto and made me content in my heart to lose goods, land, and life too, rather than swear against my conscience, and has also put in the King towards me that good and gracious mind that as yet he has taken from me nothing but my liberty with which, so help me God, his grace has done me so much good by the spiritual profit that I trust I take thereby, that among all his great benefits heaped on me so thick, I reckon, upon my faith, my imprisonment even the very chief. I cannot, I say, mistrust the grace of God, but that either he shall conserve and keep the King in that gracious mind still, to do me no hurt, or else if his pleasure be that (for my other sins) I shall suffer in such a cause in sight as I shall not deserve, his grace shall give me that strength to take it patiently, and peradventure somewhat gladly too.

Finally, Margaret, this I know very well that without my fault God will not let me be lost. I shall therefore with good hope commit myself wholly to him. And if he suffer me for my faults to perish yet shall I then serve for a praise of his justice. But in good faith, Meg, I trust that his tender pity shall keep my poor soul safe and make me commend his mercy. And therefore, mine own good daughter, never trouble thy mind, for anything that ever shall keep me in this world. Nothing can come but that which God wills. And I make myself very sure that whatever that be, seem it never so bad in sight, it shall in deed be best.

Sir Thomas More (1478–1535)

Thanksgiving after adoption

God our Father,
  giver of life and breath,
maker of all that is living,
we praise you for the wonder and joy of creation.
We thank you for the gift of this child,
and for the privilege of parenthood.
Bless our family and our life together.
Help us to be trustworthy parents.
Make us patient and understanding,
both firm and gentle,
that our child may grow up secure
in the knowledge of our love.   Anonymous

De puero balbutiente

Methinks 'tis pretty sport to hear a child
  Rocking a word in mouth yet undefiled;
The tender racquet rudely plays the sound
Which, weakly bandied, cannot back rebound;
And the soft air the softer roof doth kiss
With a sweet dying and a pretty miss,
Which hears no answer yet from the white rank
Of teeth not risen from their coral bank.
The alphabet is searched for letters soft
To try a word before it can be wrought;
And when it slideth forth, it goes as nice
As when a man doth walk upon the ice.

Thomas Bastard (1566–1618)

[43]

The first tooth

Through the house what busy joy,
  Just because the infant boy
Has a tiny tooth to show!
I have got a double row,
All as white, and all as small;
Yet no one cares for mine at all.
He can say but half a word,
Yet that single sound's preferred
To all the words that I can say
In the longest summer day.
He cannot walk, yet if he put
With mimic motion out his foot,
As if he thought he were advancing,
It's prized more than my best dancing.

Charles Lamb (1775–1834) and Mary Lamb (1764–1847)

A mother to her walking infant

Now in thy dazzling half-oped eye,
   Thy curlèd nose and lip awry,
Thy up-hoist arms and noddling head,
And little chin with crystal spread,
Poor helpless thing! what do I see,
   That I should sing of thee?

From thy poor tongue no accents come,
Which can but rub thy toothless gum;
Small understanding boasts thy face.
Thy shapeless limbs nor step nor grace;
A few short words thy feats may tell.
   And yet I love thee well.

When sudden wakes the bitter shriek,
And redder swells thy little cheek;
When rattled keys thy woes beguile,
And through the wet eye gleams the smile,
Still for thy weakly self is spent
   Thy little silly plaint.

But when thy friends are in distess,
Thou'lt laugh and chuckle ne'er the less;
Nor e'en with sympathy be smitten,
Though all are sad but thee and kitten;
Yet little varlet that thou art,
   Thou twitchest at the heart.

Thy rosy cheek so soft and warm;
Thy pinky hand and dimpled arm;
Thy silken locks that scantly peep,
With gold-tipped ends, where circles deep
Around thy neck in harmless grace
So soft and sleekly hold their place,
Might harder hearts with kindness fill,
    And gain our right good will.

Each passing clown bestows his blessing,
Thy mouth is worn with old wives' kissing:
E'en lighter looks the gloomy eye
Of surly sense, when thou art by;
And yet I think whoe'er they be,
    They love thee not like me.

Perhaps when time shall add a few
Short years to thee, thou'lt love me too.
Then wilt thou through life's weary way
Become my sure and cheering stay:
Wilt care for me, and be my hold,
    When I am weak and old.

Thou'lt listen to my lengthened tale,
And pity me when I am frail –
But see, the sweepy spinning fly
Upon the window takes thine eye,
Go to thy little senseless play –
    Thou dost not heed my lay.

Joanna Baillie (1762–1851)

Baptism

The baptism of Jesus

Jesus came from Galilee to John at the river Jordan, to be baptized by him. John would have prevented him, saying, 'I need to be baptized by you, and do you come to me?' But Jesus answered him, 'Let it be so for now; for it is proper for us in this way to fulfil all righteousness.' Then he consented. And when Jesus had been baptized, just as he came up from the water, suddenly the heavens were opened to him and he saw the Spirit of God descending like a dove and alighting on him. And a voice from heaven said, 'This is my Son, the Beloved, with whom I am well pleased.'

St Matthew's Gospel 3.13–17, the Bible

God be in my head

God be in my head,
and in my understanding;

God be in mine eyes,
and in my looking;

God be in my mouth,
and in my speaking;

God be in my heart,
and in my loving;

God be at mine end,
and at my departing.　　*Sarum Primer* (1514)

[49]

My baptismal birthday

God's child in Christ adopted – Christ my all –
　　What that earth boasts were not lost cheaply,
　　　　rather
Than forfeit that blest name, by which I call
The Holy One, the Almighty God, my Father? –
Father! In Christ we live, and Christ in thee –
Eternal Thou, and everlasting we.
The heir of heaven, henceforth I fear not death:
In Christ I live! In Christ I draw the breath
Of the true life! – Let, then, earth, sea, and sky
Make war against me! On my front I show
Their mighty Master's seal. In vain they try
To end my life, that can but end its woe.
Is that a deathbed where a Christian lies? –
Yes! But not his – 'tis death itself that dies.

Samuel Taylor Coleridge (1772–1834)

The meaning of baptism

Baptism is not an offer made by man to God, but an offer made by Christ to man. It is grounded solely in the will of Jesus Christ, as expressed in his gracious call. Baptism is essentially passive – *being baptized,* suffering the call of Christ. In baptism we become Christ's own possession. When the name of Christ is spoken over a candidate, he or she becomes a partaker in this Name, and is baptized 'into Jesus Christ'. From that moment we belong to Jesus Christ. We are wrested from the dominion of the world, and pass into the ownership of Christ.

Dietrich Bonhoeffer (1906–45)

Let the children come to me

People were bringing little children to him in order that he might touch them; and when the disciples saw it, they spoke sternly to them. But when Jesus saw this, he was indignant with the disciples and said, 'Let the little children come to me; do not stop them. For it is to such as these that the kingdom of God belongs. Truly I tell you, whoever does not receive the kingdom of God like a little child will never enter it.' And he took them up in his arms, laid his hands on them, and blessed them.

St Mark's Gospel 10.13–16, the Bible

The Lamb

Little Lamb, who made thee?
　　Dost thou know who made thee?
Gave thee life, and bid thee feed
By the stream and o'er the mead;
Gave thee clothing of delight,
Softest clothing, woolly, bright;
Gave thee such a tender voice,
Making all the vales rejoice?
　　Little Lamb, who made thee?
　　Dost thou know who made thee?

　　Little Lamb, I'll tell thee,
　　Little Lamb, I'll tell thee:
He is called by thy name,
For he calls himself a Lamb.
He is meek, and he is mild;
He became a little child.
I a child, and thou a lamb,
We are called by his name.
　　Little Lamb, God bless thee!
　　Little Lamb, God bless thee!

William Blake (1757–1827)

Trusting in the providential care of God

Throughout your life, learn to trust in the providential care of God, through which alone comes contentment. Work hard, but always to cooperate with God's good designs. Let me assure you, if you trust all to God, whatever happens will be the best for you, whether at the time it seems good or bad to your own judgement. Learn to imitate little children who, while hanging onto their father with one hand, like to gather strawberries or blackberries from the hedgerow with their free hand. In the same way, you too, whilst gathering and handling the affairs of life with one hand, must be sure that you are holding on to your heavenly Father with your other hand, looking at him from time to time to ensure that your actions and decisions are pleasing to him. Above all, make sure you never let go, or preferring to gather more things along the way, you end up falling flat on your face.

In so doing, God will work with you and in you and for you throughout your life. And at the last you will know that you have not laboured in vain, and be filled with a profound contentment which only God can give.

St Francis de Sales (1567–1622),
Introduction to a Devout Life

Learn from the child in your midst

An argument arose among the disciples as to which of them was the greatest. But Jesus, aware of their inner thoughts, took a little child and put him by his side, and said to them, 'Whoever welcomes this child in my name welcomes me, and whoever welcomes me welcomes the One who sent me; for the least among all of you is the greatest.'

St Luke's Gospel 9.46–48, the Bible

Choosing a name

I have got a new-born sister;
I was nigh the first that kissed her.
When the nursing woman brought her
To papa, his infant daughter,
How papa's dear eyes did glisten! –
She will shortly be to christen:
And papa has made me the offer,
I shall have the naming of her.

Now I wonder what would please her,
Charlotte, Julia, or Louisa.
Ann and Mary, they're too common;
Joan's too formal for a woman;
Jane's a prettier name beside;
But we had a Jane that died.
They would say, if 'twas Rebecca,
That she was a little Quaker.

Edith's pretty, but that looks
Better in old English books;
Ellen's left off long ago;
Blanche is out of fashion now.
None that I have named as yet
Are so good as Margaret.
Emily is neat and fine,
What do you think of Caroline?
How I'm puzzled and perplexed
What to choose or think of next!
I am in a little fever.
Lest the name that I shall give her
Should disgrace her or defame her,
I will leave papa to name her.

Charles Lamb (1775–1834) and Mary Lamb (1764–1847)

A prayer of St Paul

I bow my knees before the Father, from whom every
family in heaven and on earth takes its name. I pray
that, according to the riches of his glory, he may grant
you may be strengthened in your inner being with power
through his Spirit, and that Christ may dwell in your
hearts through faith, as you are being rooted and
grounded in love. I pray that you may have the power to
comprehend, with all the saints, what is the breadth and
length and height and depth, and to know the love of
Christ that surpasses knowledge, so that you may be
filled with all the fullness of God.

St Paul's Letter to the Ephesians 3.14–19, the Bible

To C. F. H. on her Christening-Day

Fair Caroline, I wonder what
   You think of earth as a dwelling-spot,
And if you'd rather have come, or not?

Today has laid on you a name
That, though unasked for, you will claim
Lifelong, for love or praise or blame.

May chance and change impose on you
No heavier burthen than this new
Care-chosen one of your future through!
Dear stranger here, the prayer is mine
That your experience may combine
Good things with glad. . . . Yes, Caroline!

Thomas Hardy (1840–1928)

A Gaelic baptism blessing

O God, who inhabits the heights,
    Come down today to my child,
The child of my body,
And bestow upon him your blessing.

In the name of the Father of peace,
When the priest of the King
Pours on him the water of meaning,
Grant my child the blessing of the Trinity
        who fills the heights,
The blessing of the One
        who fills the heights.

Sprinkle upon him your grace.
May his spirit grow strong.
Guide him in his journey through life.
Give him flocks and food.
Make him honest and true, a man without guile.
May the wisdom of the angels surround him,
So that when his life is done,
He may stand in your presence without reproach.
May he stand in your presence without reproach.

Carmina Gadelica

A prayer for success

Lord, behold our family here assembled.
   We thank thee for this place in which we dwell;
      for the love that unites us;
For the peace accorded us this day; for the hope with
      which we expect the morrow;
For the health, the work, the food, and the bright skies,
      that make our lives delightful;
For our friends in all parts of the earth;
Purge out of every heart the lurking grudge.
Give us grace and strength to forbear and to persevere.
Forgetful ourselves, help us to bear cheerfully the
      forgetfulness of others.
Give us courage and gaiety and a quiet mind.
Spare to us our friends, soften to us our enemies.
Bless us, if it may be, in all our innocent endeavours.
If it may not, give us the strength to encounter that
      which is to come,
That we may be brave in peril, constant in tribulation,
      temperate in wrath,
And in all changes of fortune,
      and down to the gates of death,
Loyal and loving one to another.
As the clay to the potter, as the windmill to the wind,
We beseech of thee this help and mercy,
      for Christ's sake.

Robert Louis Stevenson (1850–94), from his memorial by
Augustus Saint-Gaudens in St Giles' Cathedral, Edinburgh

An ancient Hebridean blessing of the family

The strength of the Triune God be our shield
    in distress,
The strength of Christ, his peace and his Pasch,
The strength of the Spirit, physician of health,
And of the precious Father, the King of grace.

Bless ourselves and our children,
Bless every one who shall come from our loins,
Bless him whose name we bear,
Bless, O God, her from whose womb we came.

Every holiness, blessing and power,
Be yielded to us every time and every hour,
In name of the Holy Threefold above,
Father, Son and Spirit everlasting.

Be the cross of Christ to shield us downward,
Be the cross of Christ to shield us upward,
Be the cross of Christ to shield us roundward,
Accepting our Beltane blessing from us,
Accepting our Beltane blessing from us.

From an ancient 'Beltane Blessing', *Carmina Gadelica*
(Beltane is 1 May)

Lord of all hopefulness

Lord of all hopefulness, Lord of all joy,
  Whose trust, ever child-like,
    no cares could destroy,
Be there at our waking, and give us, we pray,
Your bliss in our hearts, Lord, at the break of the day.

Lord of all eagerness, Lord of all faith,
Whose strong hands were skilled
  at the plane and the lathe,
Be there at our labours, and give us, we pray,
Your strength in our hearts, Lord,
  at the noon of the day.

Lord of all kindliness, Lord of all grace,
Your hands swift to welcome, your arms to embrace,
Be there at our homing, and give us, we pray,
Your love in our hearts, Lord, at the eve of the day.

Lord of all gentleness, Lord of all calm,
Whose voice is contentment, whose presence is balm,
Be there at our sleeping, and give us, we pray,
Your peace in our hearts, Lord, at the end of the day.

Jan Struther (1901–53)

Childhood

The Declaration of Geneva concerning the Rights of a Child

By the present Declaration of the Rights of the Child, commonly known as the 'Declaration of Geneva', men and women of all nations, recognising that humankind owes to the child the best that it has to give, declare and accept it as their duty, that beyond and above all considerations of race, nationality or creed:

I   THE CHILD must be given the means requisite for its normal development, both materially and spiritually.

II THE CHILD that is hungry must be fed; the child that is sick must be nursed; the child that is backward must be helped; the delinquent child must be reclaimed; and the orphan and the waif must be sheltered and succoured.

III THE CHILD must be the first to receive relief in times of distress.

IV THE CHILD must be put in a position to earn a livelihood, and must be protected against every form of exploitation.

V   THE CHILD must be brought up in the consciousness that its talents must be devoted to the service of other fellow men and women.

As adopted by The League of Nations, 1924

I remember, I remember

I remember, I remember
The house where I was born,
The little window where the sun
Came peeping in at morn;
He never came a wink too soon
Nor brought too long a day;
But now, I often wish the night
Had borne my breath away.

I remember, I remember
The roses, red and white,
The violets, and the lily-cups –
Those flowers made of light!
The lilacs where the robin built,
And where my brother set
The laburnum on his birthday –
The tree is living yet!

I remember, I remember
Where I used to swing,
And thought the air must rush as fresh
To swallows on the wing;
My spirit flew in feathers then
That is so heavy now,
And summer pools could hardly cool
The fever on my brow.

I remember, I remember
The fir trees dark and high;
I used to think their slender tops
Were close against the sky:
It was a childish ignorance,
But now 'tis little joy
To know I'm farther off from heaven
Than when I was a boy.

Thomas Hood (1799–1845)

My child, do not forget my teaching

My child, do not forget my teaching,
but let your heart keep my commandments;
for length of days and years of life
and abundant welfare they will give you.
Do not let loyalty and faithfulness forsake you;
bind them around your neck,
write them on the tablet of your heart.
So you will find favour and good repute
in the sight of God and of people.
Trust in the Lord with all your heart,
and do not rely on your own insight.
In all your ways acknowledge God,
and he will make straight your paths.

Proverbs 3.1–6, the Bible

Nurse's song

When the voices of children are heard on the green
  And laughing is heard on the hill,
My heart is at rest within my breast
And everything else is still.

'Then come home, my children, the sun is gone down
And the dews of night arise;
Come, come, leave off play, and let us away
Till the morning appears in the skies.'

'No, no, let us play, for it is yet day
And we cannot go to sleep;
Besides, in the sky the little birds fly
And the hills are all cover'd with sheep.'

'Well, well, go and play till the light fades away
And then go home to bed.'
The little ones leaped and shouted and laugh'd
And all the hills echoed.

William Blake (1757–1827), *Songs of Innocence*

A boy's song

Where the pools are bright and deep,
  Where the grey trout lies asleep,
Up the river and over the lea,
That's the way for Billy and me.

Where the blackbird sings the latest,
Where the hawthorn blooms the sweetest,
Where the nestlings chirp and flee,
That's the way for Billy and me.

Where the mowers mow the cleanest,
Where the hay lies thick and greenest,
There to track the homeward bee,
That's the way for Billy and me.

Where the hazel bank is steepest,
Where the shadow falls the deepest,
Where the clustering nuts fall free,
That's the way for Billy and me.

Why the boys should drive away
Little sweet maidens from the play,
Or love to banter and fight so well,
That's the thing I never could tell.

But this I know, I love to play
Through the meadow, among the hay;
Up the water and over the lea,
That's the way for Billy and me.

James Hogg (1770–1835)

Childhood

The past: it is a magic word,
  Too beautiful to last.
It looks back like a lovely face,
Who can forget the past?
There's music in its childhood
That's known in every tongue,
Like the music of the wildwood:
All chorus to the song.

The happy dream, the joyous play,
The life without a sigh,
The beauty thoughts can ne'er portray
In those four letters lie.
The painters beauty breathing art
The poets speaking pens
Can ne'er call back a thousand part
Of what that word contains.

John Clare (1793–1864), *Childhood* or *The Past*

There was a little girl

There was a little girl
Who had a little curl
Right in the middle of her forehead.
When she was good
She was very, very good,
But when she was bad she was horrid.

Henry Wadsworth Longfellow (1807–82)

He is our childhood's pattern

For he is our childhood's pattern,
Day by day like us he grew,
He was little, weak, and helpless,
Tears and smiles like us he knew,
And he feeleth for our sadness,
And he shareth in our gladness.

And our eyes at last shall see him,
Through his own redeeming love,
For that child so dear and gentle
Is our Lord in heaven above;
And he leads his children on
To the place where he is gone.

Cecil Frances Alexander (1818–95),
Once in Royal David's City

Ex ore infantium

Little Jesus, wast thou shy
        Once, and just so small as I?
And what did it feel like to be
Out of heaven, and just like me?
Didst thou sometimes think of *there,*
And ask where all the angels were?
I should think that I would cry
For my house all made of sky;
I would look about the air,
And wonder where my angels were;
And at waking 'twould distress me –
Not an angel there to dress me!

Hadst thou ever any toys,
Like us little girls and boys?
And didst thou play in heaven with all
The angels, that were not too tall,
With stars for marbles? Did the things
Play 'Can you see me?' through their wings?

Didst thou kneel at night to pray,
And didst thou join thy hands, this way?
And did they tire sometimes, being young,
And make the prayer seem very long?
And dost thou like it best, that we
Should join our hands to pray to thee?
I used to think, before I knew,
The prayer not said unless we do.
And did thy Mother at the night

Kiss thee, and fold the clothes in right?
And didst thou feel quite good in bed,
Kissed, and sweet, and thy prayers said?

Thou canst not have forgotten all
That it feels like to be small:
And thou know'st I cannot pray
To thee in my father's way –
When thou wast so little, say,
Couldst thou talk thy Father's way? –

So, a little Child, come down
And hear a child's tongue like thy own;
Take me by the hand and walk,
And listen to my baby-talk.
To thy Father show my prayer
(He will look, thou art so fair),
And say: 'O Father, I, thy Son,
Bring the prayer of a little one.'

And he will smile, that children's tongue
Has not changed since thou wast young!

Francis Thompson (1859–1907)

My shadow

I have a little shadow that goes in and out with me,
  And what can be the use of him is more than I can
    see.
He is very, very like me from the heels up to the head;
And I see him jump before me, when I jump into my
    bed.

The funniest thing about him is the way he likes to
    grow –
Not at all like proper children, which is always very
    slow;
For he sometimes shoots up taller like an indiarubber
    ball,
And he sometimes gets so little that there's none of him
    at all.

He hasn't got a notion of how children ought to play,
And can only make a fool of me in every sort of way.
He stays so close beside me, he's a coward you can see;
I'd think shame to stick to nursie as that shadow sticks
    to me!

One morning, very early, before the sun was up,
I rose and found the shining dew on every buttercup;
But my lazy little shadow, like an arrant sleepy-head,
Had stayed at home behind me and was fast asleep in
    bed.

Robert Louis Stevenson (1850–94)

The schoolboy

I love to rise in a summer morn
   When the birds sing on every tree;
The distant huntsman winds his horn,
And the sky-lark sings with me.
O! what sweet company.

But to go to school in a summer morn,
O! it drives all joy away;
Under a cruel eye outworn,
The little ones spend the day
In sighing and dismay.

Ah! then at times I drooping sit,
And spend many an anxious hour,
Nor in my book can I take delight,
Nor sit in learning's bower,
Worn thro' with the dreary shower.

How can the bird that is born of joy
Sit in a cage and sing?
How can a child, when fears annoy,
But droop his tender wing,
And forget his youthful spring?

O! father and mother, if buds are nip'd
And blossoms blown away,
And if the tender plants are strip'd
Of their joy in the springing day,
By sorrow ands care's dismay,

How shall the summer arise in joy,
Or the summer fruits appear?
Or how shall we gather what griefs destroy,
Or bless the mellowing year,
When the blasts of winter appear?

William Blake (1757–1827)

The blind boy

O say, what is that thing called light,
    Which I can ne'er enjoy?
What is the blessing of the sight?
    O tell your poor blind boy!

You talk of wondrous things you see,
    You say the sun shines bright;
I feel him warm, but how can he
    Then make it day or night?

My day or night myself I make
    Whene'er I sleep or play;
And could I ever keep awake
    With me 'twere always day.

With heavy sighs I often hear
    You mourn my hapless woe;
But sure with patience I may bear
    A loss I ne'er can know.

Then let not what I cannot have
My cheer of mind destroy;
Whilst thus I sing, I am a king,
Although a poor blind boy.

Colley Cibber (1671–1757)

The land of counterpane

When I was sick and lay a-bed,
I had two pillows at my head,
And all my toys beside me lay
To keep me happy all the day.

And sometimes for an hour or so
I watched my leaden soldiers go,
With different uniforms and drills,
Among the bed-clothes, through the hills;

And sometimes sent my ships in fleets
All up and down among the sheets;
Or brought my trees and houses out,
And planted cities all about.

I was the giant great and still
That sits upon the pillow-hill,
And sees before him, dale and plain,
The pleasant land of counterpane.

Robert Louis Stevenson (1850–94)

Above the bright blue sky

There's a Friend for little children
    Above the bright blue sky,
A Friend who never changes,
    Whose love will never die;
Our earthly friends may fail us,
    And change with changing years,
This Friend is always worthy
    Of that dear name he bears.

There's a home for little children
    Above the bright blue sky,
Where Jesus reigns in glory,
    A home of peace and joy;
No home on earth is like it,
    Nor can with it compare;
And everyone is happy,
    Nor could be happier there.

Albert Midlane (1825–1909)

Gust becos I cud not spel

Gust becos I cud not spel
It did not mean I was daft
When the boys in school red my riting
Some of them laffed.

But now I am the dictater
They have to rite like me
Utherwise they cannot pas
Ther GCSE

Some of the girls wer ok
But those who laffed a lot
Have al bean rownded up
And have recently bean shot

The teacher who corrected my speling
As not been shot at al
But four the last fifteen howers
As bean standing up against a wal

He has to stand ther until he can spel
Figgymisgrugifooniyn the rite way
I think he will stand ther forever
I just invented it today

Brian Patten (1946–)

How can the young find their way in this world?

How can the young find their way in this world?
By staying close to God's word.
I seek you with my whole heart:
do not let me stray from your path.
I treasure your truth, deep within my heart,
so that I should never cease to love you.
I bless you, O Lord;
teach me your wisdom.
With my lips I want to echo your judgements.
For I take greater delight in your commands
than in all manner or riches.
I will meditate on your laws,
searching out your ways.
My delight will be in your counsel,
and I will not forget your word.

Psalm 119, the Bible

Parenthood

Children learn what they live

If a child lives with criticism, she learns to condemn.
If a child lives with hostility, he learns to fight.

If a child lives with ridicule, she learns to be shy.
If a child lives with shame, he learns to feel guilty.

If a child lives with tolerance, she learns to be patient.
If a child lives with encouragement, he learns
    confidence.

If a child lives with praise, she learns to appreciate.
If a child lives with fairness, he learns justice.

If a child lives with security, she learns to have faith.
If a child lives with approval, he learns to like himself.

If children live with acceptance and friendship,
    they learn to find love in the world.

Anonymous

Giving good gifts to your children

Jesus said to his disciples, 'I say to you, Ask, and it will
be given you; search, and you will find; knock, and
the door will be opened for you. For everyone who
asks receives, and everyone who searches finds, and for
everyone who knocks, the door will be opened. Is there

anyone among you who, if your child asks for a fish, will give a snake instead of a fish? Or if the child asks for an egg, will give a scorpion? If you then, who are evil, know how to give good gifts to your children, how much more will the heavenly Father give the Holy Spirit to those who ask him!'

St Luke's Gospel 11.8–13, the Bible

The toys

My little son, who looked from thoughtful eyes
And moved and spoke in quiet grown-up wise,
Having my law the seventh time disobeyed,
I struck him, and dismissed
With hard words and unkissed,
His mother, who was patient, being dead.
Then, fearing lest his grief should hinder sleep,
I visited his bed,
But found him slumbering deep,
With darkened eyelids, and their lashes yet
From his late sobbing wet.
And I, with moan,
Kissing away his tears, left others of my own;
For, on a table drawn beside his head,
He had put, within his reach,
A box of counters and a red-veined stone,
A piece of glass abraded by the beach
And six or seven shells,
A bottle with bluebells

And two French copper coins, ranged there with
   careful art,
To comfort his sad heart.
So when that night I prayed
To God, I wept, and said:
Ah, when at last we die with trancèd breath,
Not vexing Thee in death,
And Thou rememberest of what toys
We made our joys,
How weakly understood,
Thy great commanded good,
Then, fatherly not less
Than I whom Thou has moulded from the clay,
Thou'lt leave Thy wrath, and say,
'I will be sorry for their childishness.'

Coventry Patmore (1823–96)

Dombey and Son

Dombey sat in the corner of the darkened room in
the great armchair by the bedside, and Son lay
tucked up warm in a little basket bedstead, carefully
disposed on a low settee immediately in front of the fire
and close to it, as if his constitution were analogous to
that of a muffin, and it was essential to toast him brown
while he was very new.

Dombey was about eight-and-forty years of age. Son
about eight-and-forty minutes. Dombey was rather bald,

rather red, and though a handsome well-made man, too stern and pompous in appearance to be prepossessing. Son was very bald, and very red, and though (of course) an undeniably fine infant, somewhat crushed and spotty in his general effect, as yet. On the brow of Dombey, Time and his brother Care had set some marks, as on a tree that was to come down in good time – remorseless twins they are for striding through their human forests, notching as they go – while the countenance of Son was crossed with a thousand little creases, which the same deceitful Time would take delight in smoothing out and wearing away with the flat part of his scythe, as a preparation of the surface for his deeper operations.

Dombey, exulting in the long-looked-for event, jingled and jingled the heavy gold watch-chain that depended from below his trim blue coat, whereof the buttons sparkled phosphorescently in the feeble rays of the distant fire. Son, with his little fists curled up and clenched, seemed, in his feeble way, to be squaring at existence for having come upon him so unexpectedly.

Charles Dickens (1812–70), *Dombey and Son*

The children's hour

Between the dark and the daylight,
        When the night is beginning to lower,
Comes a pause in the day's occupations,
        That is known as the Children's Hour.

I hear in the chamber above me
        The patter of little feet,
The sound of a door that is opened,
        And voices soft and sweet.

From my study I see in the lamplight,
        Descending the broad hall stair,
Alice, and laughing Allegra,
        And Edith with golden hair.

A whisper, and then a silence:
        Yet I know by their merry eyes
They are plotting and planning together
        To take me by surprise.

A sudden rush from the stairway,
        A sudden raid from the hall!
By three doors left unguarded
        They enter my castle wall!

They climb up into my turret
        O'er the arms and back of my chair;
If I try to escape, they surround me;
        They seem to be everywhere.

They almost devour me with kisses,
      Their arms about me entwine,
Till I think of the Bishop of Bingen
      In his Mouse-Tower on the Rhine!

Do you think, O blue-eyed banditti,
      Because you have scaled the wall,
Such an old moustache as I am
      Is not a match for you all!

I have you fast in my fortress,
      And will not let you depart,
But put you down into the dungeon
      In the round-tower of my heart.

And there will I keep you forever,
      Yes, forever and a day,
Till the walls shall crumble to ruin,
      And moulder in dust away!

Henry Wadsworth Longfellow (1807–82)

Children

Your children are not your children. They are sons and daughters of Life's longing for itself. They come through you but not from you. And though they are with you, yet they belong not to you.

You may give them your love, but not your thoughts,
for they have their own thoughts.

You may house their bodies, but not their souls, for
their souls dwell in the house of tomorrow, which you
cannot visit, not even in your dreams.

You may strive to be like them, but seek not to make
them like you. For life goes not backward nor tarries
with yesterday.

You are the bows from which your children as living
arrows are sent forth. The archer sees the mark upon
the path of the infinite, and he bends you with his might
that his arrows may go swift and far. Let your bending
in the archer's hand be for gladness; for even as he loves
the arrow that flies, so he loves also the bow that is
stable.

Khalil Gibran (1883–1931), *The Prophet*

I will show you beauty

Come my son,
   to see the reasons why you were conceived
to know why you happened.
I will show you the beauty of the breath breathed into
   you,
I will show you the world
that is a richness of acres between your feet.

Come, my son,
I will show you the sheep
that keep the Gwryd tidy with their kisses,
the cow and her calf in Cefn Llan,
foxgloves and bluebells
and honeysuckle on a hedgerow in Rhyd-y-fro;

I will show you how to fashion
a whistle from the twigs of the great sycamore-tree
in the incomparable woods of John Bifan,
how to look for nests on the slopes of Barli Bach,
how to swim naked in the river;

I will show you the thick undergrowth
between Ifan's farm and the grey Vicarage,
where the blackberries are legion
and the chestnuts still on the floor;

I will show you the bilberries thick
on the scattered clumps of mountain moss;

I will show you the toad
in the damp dusk,
and the old workings beneath the growing hay;

I will show you the house where Gwenallt was born.

Come, my son,
in your father's hand,
and I will show you the beauty
that lives in your mother's blue eyes.

Dafydd Rowlands

Let us love one another

Let us love one another, because love is from God; everyone who loves is born of God and knows God. Whoever does not love does not know God, for God is love. God's love was revealed among us in this way: God sent his only Son into the world so that we might live through him. In this is love, not that we loved God but that he loved us and sent his Son to be the atoning sacrifice for our sins. Beloved, since God loved us so much, we also ought to love one another. No one has ever seen God: if we love one another, God lives in us, and his love is perfected in us.

God is love, and those who abide in love abide in God, and God abides in them. There is no fear in love, but perfect love casts out fear.

First Letter of St John 4, the Bible

On the beach at night

On the beach at night,
   Stands a child with her father,
Watching the east, the autumn sky.

Up through the darkness,
While ravening clouds, the burial clouds, in black
   masses spreading,
Lower sullen and fast athwart and down the sky,

Amid a transparent clear belt of ether yet left in the east,
Ascends large and calm the lord-star Jupiter,
And nigh at hand, only a very little above,
Swim the delicate sisters the Pleiades.

From the beach the child holding the hand of her father,
Those burial-clouds that lower victorious soon to
    devour all,
Watching, silently weeps.

Weep not, child,
Weep not, my darling,
With these kisses let me remove your tears,
The ravening clouds shall not long be victorious,
They shall not long possess the sky, they devour the
    stars only in apparition,
Jupiter shall emerge, be patient, watch again another
    night, the Pleiades shall emerge,
They are immortal, all those stars both silvery and
    golden shall shine out again,
The great stars and the little ones shall shine out again,
    they endure.
The vast immortal suns and the long-enduring pensive
    moons shall again shine.

Then dearest child, mournest thou only for Jupiter?
Considerest thou alone the burial of the stars?

Something there is,
(With my lips soothing thee, adding I whisper,
I give thee the first suggestion, the problem and
    indirection,)
Something there is more immortal even than the stars,
(Many the burials, many the days and nights, passing
    away,)
Something that shall endure longer even than lustrous
    Jupiter,
Longer than sun or any revolving satellite,
Or the radiant sisters the Pleiades.

Walt Whitman (1819–92)

The peace of wild things

When despair for the world grows in me
    and I wake in the night at the least sound
in fear of what my life and my children's lives may be,
I go and lie down where the wood drake
rests in his beauty on the water, and the great heron
    feeds.
I come into the peace of wild things
who do not tax their lives with forethought
of grief. I come into the presence of still water.
And I feel above me the day-blind stars
waiting with their light. For a time
I rest in the grace of the world, and am free.

Wendell Berry (1934–)

On my first son
An Epitaph

Farewell, thou child of my right hand, and joy;
My sin was too much hope of thee, loved boy:
Seven years thou 'wert lent to me, and I thee pay,
Exacted by thy fate, on the just day.
O could I lose all father now! For why
Will man lament the state he should envy,
To have so soon 'scaped world's and flesh's rage,
And, if no other misery, yet age?
Rest in soft peace, and asked, say, 'Here doth lie
Ben Johnson his best piece of poetry.'
For whose sake henceforth all his vows be such
As what he loves may never like too much.

Ben Jonson (1572–1637)

On my first daughter
An Epitaph

Here lies to each her parents' ruth
  Mary, the daughter of their youth:
Yet, all heaven's gifts being heaven's due,
It makes the father less to rue.
At six months' end she parted hence
With safety of her innocence
Whose soul heaven's Queen (whose name she bears)
In comfort of her mother's tears,
Hath placed amongst her virgin-train;
Where, while that severed doth remain,
This grave partakes the fleshly birth,
Which cover lightly, gentle earth.

Ben Jonson (1572–1637)

Young and old

When all the world is young, lad,
    And all the trees are green;
And every goose a swan, lad,
    And every lass a queen;
Then hey for boot and horse, lad,
    And round the world away;
Young blood must have its course, lad,
    And every dog his day.

When all the world is old, lad,
    And all the trees are brown;
When all the sport is stale, lad,
    And all the wheels run down;
Creep home, and take your place there,
    The spent and maimed among:
God grant you find one face there,
    You loved when all was young.

Charles Kingsley (1819–75)

Piano

Softly, in the dusk, a woman is singing to me:
   Taking me back down the vista of years, till I see
A child sitting under the piano, in the boom of the
   tingling strings
And pressing the small, poised feet of a mother who
   smiles as she sings.

In spite of myself, the insidious mastery of song
Betrays me back, till the heart of me weeps to belong
To the old Sunday evenings at home, with winter
   outside
And hymns in the cosy parlour, the tinking piano
   our guide.

So now it is vain for the singer to burst into clamour
With the great black piano appassionato. The glamour
Of childish days is upon me, my manhood is cast
Down in the flood of remembrance, I weep like a child
   for the past.

D. H. Lawrence (1885–1930)

Youth is a state of mind

Youth is not a time of life . . . it is a state of mind. Nobody grows old by merely living a number of years; people grow old only by deserting their ideals. Years wrinkle the skin, but to give up enthusiasm wrinkles the soul. Worry, doubt, self-distrust, fear and despair, these turn the long, long years that bow the head and turn the growing spirit back to dust.

Whether seventy or sixteen, there is in every being's heart the love of wonder, the sweet amazement at the stars and the starlike things and thoughts, the undaunted challenge of events, and unfailing childlike appetite for what next, and the joy of the game of life.

You are as young as your faith, as old as your doubt; as young as your self-confidence, as old as your fear; as young as your hope, as old as your despair.

Anonymous

If

If you can keep your head when all about you
     Are losing theirs and blaming it on you;
If you can trust yourself when all men doubt you,
But make allowance for their doubting too;
If you can wait and not be tired by waiting,
Or being lied about, don't deal in lies,

Or being hated, don't give way to hating,
And yet don't look too good, nor talk too wise:

If you can dream – and not make dreams your master;
If you can think – and not make thoughts your aim;
If you can meet with Triumph and Disaster
And treat those two imposters just the same;
If you can bear to hear the truth you've spoken
Twisted by knaves to make a trap for fools,
Or watch the things you gave your life to, broken,
And stoop and build 'em up with worn-out tools;

If you can make one heap of all your winnings
And risk it on one turn of pitch-and-toss,
And lose, and start again at your beginnings
And never breathe a word about your loss;
If you can force your heart and nerve and sinew
To serve your turn long after they are gone,
And so hold on when there is nothing in you
Except the Will which says to them: 'Hold on!'

If you can talk with crowds and keep your virtue,
Or walk with kings – nor lose the common touch,
If neither foes nor loving friends can hurt you,
If all men count with you, but none too much;
If you can fill the unforgiving minute
With sixty seconds' worth of distance run –
Yours is the Earth and everything that's in it,
And – which is more – you'll be a Man, my son!

Rudyard Kipling (1865–1936)

Letter to Billy Elliot
from his mother written just before her death,
to be read on his 18th birthday

To my son

Dear Billy

I know I must seem like a distant memory to you, which is probably a good thing. It will have been a long time, and I will have missed seeing you grow. I will have missed your crying, your loving, your shopping. And I will have missed telling you off.

But please know that I was always there with you through everything. I always will be. And I am proud to have known you, and I am proud that you were mine. Always be yourself.

I love you for ever.

Mum

Lee Hall, screenplay of *Billy Elliot*

The Lord's my Shepherd

The Lord's my Shepherd, I'll not want,
    He makes me down to lie
In pastures green; he leadeth me
The quiet waters by.

My soul he doth restore again,
And me to walk doth make
Within the paths of righteousness,
E'en for his own name's sake.

Yea, though I walk through death's dark vale
Yet will I fear no ill;
For thou art with me, and thy rod
And staff me comfort still.

My table thou hast furnished
In presence of my foes;
My head thou dost with oil anoint,
And my cup overflows.

Goodness and mercy all my life
Shall surely follow me;
And in God's house for evermore
My dwelling-place shall be.

Psalm 23, Scottish paraphrase (1650)

For Andrew

'Will I die?' you ask. And so I enter on
The dutiful exposition of that which you
Would rather not know, and I rather not tell you.
To soften my 'Yes' I offer compensations –
Age and fulfilment ('It's so far away;
You will have children and grandchildren by then')
And indifference ('By then you will not care').
No need: you cannot believe me, convinced
That if you always eat plenty of vegetables
And are careful crossing the street you will live for ever.
And so we close the subject, with much unsaid –
This, for instance: Though you and I may die
Tomorrow or next year, and nothing remain
Of our stock, of the unique, preciously-hoarded
Inimitable genes we carry in us,
It is possible that for many generations
There will exist, sprung from whatever seeds,
Children straight-limbed, with clear enquiring voices,
Bright-eyed as you. Or so I like to think:
Sharing in this your childish optimism.

Fleur Adcock (1934–)

Walking away
For Sean

It is eighteen years ago, almost to the day –
  A sunny day with the leaves just turning,
The touch-lines new-ruled – since I watched you play
Your first game of football, then, like a satellite
Wrenched from its orbit, go drifting away

Behind a scatter of boys. I can see
You walking away from me towards the school
With the pathos of a half-fledged thing set free
Into a wilderness, the gait of one
Who finds no path where the path should be.

That hesitant figure, eddying away
Like a winged seed loosened from its parent stem,
Has something I never quite grasp to convey
About nature's give-and-take – the small, the scorching
Ordeals which fire one's irresolute clay.

I have had worse partings, but none that so
Gnaws at my mind still. Perhaps it is roughly
Saying what God alone could perfectly show –
How selfhood begins with a walking away,
And love is proved in the letting go.

C. Day Lewis (1904–72)

Learn to be gentle with yourselves, not simply with your children

One form of gentleness that we should all practise is towards ourselves. We should not get irritable with ourselves, fretting at our imperfections. It is natural to be upset and feel sorry when we have done something wrong, but we should refrain from being full of self-recrimination, fretful or spiteful to ourselves.

Some people make the great mistake of being angry with others because they have been the recipient of anger, hurt because they have been hurt themselves, vexed because they have allowed themselves to be vexed. They think that they are getting rid of their anger, that the second remedies the first; but actually, they are trapped in a destructive cycle of behaviour which will come to the surface in fresh outbursts of anger on a later occasion.

Besides this, irritation and anger with ourselves tends to foster pride, and springs from a form of self-love which is then disconcerted and upset at discovering that we are not perfect after all. We should regard our faults with calm, collected and firm displeasure. Just as a judge, when sentencing a criminal, functions much better when guided by reason, conducting the proceedings with tranquillity, and not allowing himself to have an emotional or violent response to the case; so too we will correct ourselves better by a quiet persevering self-examination rather than by an irritated, hasty and passionate one. Repentance generated by anger tends to be disproportionate to our faults, and controlled by our inner compulsions.

When your heart has fallen, raise it up softly, gently, humbling yourself before God, acknowledging your fault, but without being surprised at your fall.

St Francis de Sales (1567–1622),
Introduction to a Devout Life

When I was a child

Love is patient; love is kind; love is not envious or boastful or arrogant or rude. It does not insist on its own way; it is not irritable or resentful; it does not rejoice in wrongdoing, but rejoices in the truth. It bears all things, believes all things, hopes all things, endures all things.

Love never ends. But as for prophecies, they will come to an end; as for tongues, they will cease; as for knowledge, it will come to an end. For we know only in part, and we prophesy only in part; but when the complete comes, the partial will come to an end.

When I was a child, I spoke like a child, I thought like a child, I reasoned like a child; when I became an adult, I put an end to childish ways. For now we see in a mirror, dimly, but then we will see face to face. Now I know only in part; then I will know fully, even as I have been fully known. And now faith, hope and live abide, these three; but the greatest of these is love.

St Paul's First Letter to the Corinthians 13.4–13, the Bible

The human family

Swiftly arose and spread around me the peace and joy and
knowledge that pass all the art and argument of the earth;
And I know that the hand of God is the elderhand of my own,
And I know that the spirit of God is the eldest brother of my own,
And that all the men ever born are also my brothers, and the women my sisters and lovers.

Walt Whitman (1819–92), *Song of myself*

A farewell

My fairest child, I have no song to give you;
    No lark could pipe to skies so dull and grey:
Yet, ere we part, one lesson I can leave you
        For every day.

Be good, sweet maid, and let who will be clever;
        Do noble things, not dream them, all day long:
And so make life, death, and the vast forever
        One grand, sweet song.

Charles Kingsley (1819–75)

Acknowledgements

Where no acknowledgement is made in the anthology, no source or author is known. Every effort has been made to trace copyright ownership of items included in this anthology. The Author and Publishers apologise to those who have not been traced at the time of going to press, and whose rights who have inadvertently not been acknowledged. They would be grateful to be informed of any omissions or inaccuracies in this respect. The Author and Publisher are grateful for permission to reproduce material under copyright, and are grateful to the following copyright holders:

The Society of Authors, acting on behalf of the Literary Trustees for the late Walter de la Mare, for his poem, 'The Birthnight'.

Beth Bentley, 'The Birthing', *Phone Calls from the Dead,* University of Ohio Press, 1970.

Bloodaxe Books Ltd, for Fleur Adcock's poem, 'For Andrew', *Selected Poems*, 1983;

Judy Daish Associates, for an extract from Lee Hall's screenplay, *Billy Elliot* © Lee Hall;

Gomer Press, for Dafydd Rowlands' poem, 'I will show

you Beauty', *Meini,* the original collection of Dafydd
Rowland's poetry, and subsequently translated from
the Welsh by R. Gerallt Jones in *Poetry of Wales
1930–1970,* edited by R. Gerallt Jones; both editions
published by Gomer Press.

David Higham Associates, for an extract from *Under
Milk Wood,* Dylan Thomas, J. M. Dent.

The Estate of C. Day Lewis for his poem, 'Walking
Away', *The Complete Poems,* Sinclair-Stevenson,
1992 © 1992 in this edition and the estate of C. Day
Lewis.

North Point Press, a division of Farrar, Straus & Giroux,
LLC., for Wendell Berry's poem, 'The Peace of Wild
Things', *Collected Poems 1957–1982* ©1985, Wendell
Berry.

Ohio University Press, jointly with the estate of J. V.
Cunningham, for his poem 'Dear Child Whom I
Begot', *The Poems of J. V. Cunningham,* 1998, pub-
lished jointly with Swallow Press, Ohio.

Oxford University Press, for the text of Jan Struther's
hymn, 'Lord of all hopefulness'.

Penguin Ltd, for an extract from Fergal Keane, *Letter to
Daniel,* 1996.

Rogers, Coleridge and White, for Brian Patten's poem,
'Gust Becos I Cud Not Spel', *Gargling with Jelly,*
Viking, 1985 © Brian Patten, 1985.

SCM-Canterbury Press Ltd, for an extract from *The
Cost of Discipleship,* Dietrich Bonhoeffer, ET by R. H.
Fuller, 1948; for Cecily Taylor's poem, 'New Arrival';
Anne Richards' poem, 'Lovesong'; and Andrew Pratt's

poem, 'Gentle Whisper, Hardly Crying'; all from *Lifetime of Blessing*, 2005.

Texas Tech University Press, for Shelly Wagner's poem, 'Birth of a Child' *The Andrew Poems*; © Shelly Wagner, 1991.

Weidenfeld & Nicholson Ltd, a division of the Orion Group, for an extract from Margaret Drabble, *The Millstone*, London, 1965.

Index of Biblical Readings

Apart from the psalms which are in a version of the author, all quotations are taken from the *New Revised Standard Version* © 1989 The Division of Christian Education of the National Council of Churches in the USA.

Index of Authors

[109]

Index of Titles or First Lines